*Now may the God of peace himself sanctify you completely, and may your whole spirit and soul and body be kept blameless at the coming of our Lord Jesus Christ.*

1 THESSALONIANS 5:23

# Celebrate Salvation!®

# Sanctified
# Coming Clean with God

### Stage B - Living in the Word and the World

*The Joy of Christian Discipleship Series*
*Book 2*

## Dr. Bill Morehouse

His Kingdom Press

# About Dr. Bill Morehouse

Dr. Morehouse was raised in a traditional Christian home in the 1950's and functionally became a humanist during college and medical school in the 1960's. After completing his medical residency in Family Medicine in the early 1970's he embarked on a career of serving the poor but soon found that his secular faith and alternative lifestyle were woefully inadequate to the task.

In 1974 he underwent a dramatic conversion from the philosophy and lifestyle he had been living to a wholehearted commitment to Jesus as his LORD and Savior. After returning to medicine and marrying in 1975, he and his wife have dedicated themselves to growing in faith, raising their family of four children (plus spouses and grandchildren), and providing Christ-centered service to some of the most disadvantaged members of their community.

Since retiring from active clinical practice in July 2018, Dr. Morehouse has devoted himself to continued Christian growth, study, writing, and teaching about the Kingdom of God. He has had long personal and professional experience with the material covered in Celebrate Salvation.®

*Sanctified: Coming Clean with God*
Copyright 2020 by William R. Morehouse
ISBN: 978-1-7353899-2-9 (paperback)
Web Address: www.celebratesalvation.org

 **His Kingdom Press**
Rochester, New York 14619

Special discounts are available on quantity purchases by corporations, associations, educators, and others. For details, contact the publisher through www.hiskingdom.us/press.

# Sanctified Contents

## Background Material

## Sanctified: Coming Clean with God

# Acknowledgements

The work you have in your hands is part of a collaboration with roots that extend back for generations and even millennia. Jesus came to reveal God's love to struggling mankind and to demonstrate the depth of that love in ways that have had a profound impact on countless lives ever since. He embodied the fullness of God in human form and called us out of darkness, confusion, and bondage into the wonderful light, clarity, and freedom we were created to inhabit.

We appear to start out so fresh and pure as infants but soon become soiled and spoiled. Then as the years go by we get deeper and deeper in. As the Psalmist wrote:

> *The LORD looks down from heaven on the children of man, to see if there are any who understand, who seek after God. They have all turned aside; together they have become corrupt; there is none who does good, not even one.*
>
> Psalm 14:2-3, also noted in Psalm 53:1-3 and Romans 3:10-12

How can we come clean? Do you believe in second, third, and even seven times seventieth chances? God does.

Historically, there were entire eras when certain troubling human conditions, like addictions and criminal behavior, were just written off as hopeless. This work owes a deep debt of ongoing gratitude, first to the God who saves and then to fellow believers in the Body of Christ who are working tirelessly to reveal and share the truth that God hears our prayers and has life-giving answers for even our most challenging and "unsolvable" problems.

Many people are continuing to contribute their prayers, thoughts, ideas, and constructive comments to the growth and development of Celebrate Salvation.® I am particularly grateful for the pioneering work of John Baker, Rick Warren, and their colleagues at Saddleback Church as well as to many contributors in my local church fellowship and beyond. I would especially like to honor my wife and life partner, Susan, for her unfailing love and support over the decades we have been given to share life, faith, family, and community together.

# Meeting 21ˢᵗ Century Needs

**C**elebrate Salvation® has developed a broad-based Christ-centered study series and discipleship program designed to reach a wide audience of sincere seekers. Are you searching for truth in our troubled age, a new believer seeking to be grounded, someone who has recently renewed your faith commitment in Christ and wants to revitalize your faith and ability to be an effective witness to others, or a church leader committed to growth? If so, this course is for you.

Celebrate Salvation's® underlying design is based on a set of several Biblical understandings first clearly outlined during the Oxford Group revival in the early 20ᵗʰ Century. One outgrowth of this movement became the time-honored 12-Steps and Traditions of Alcoholics Anonymous which have been instrumental in helping millions find God-given strength to overcome addictive behaviors. However, since then many 12-step recovery programs have revised their terminology to reach people who've had negative experiences with organized religion by replacing references to "God" with the term "a higher power" which is left up to each participant to define.

In the 1990s the 12-Step approach was significantly reframed by John Baker and Rick Warren at Saddleback Church into a clearly Christian program compatible with its Oxford Group roots. Following the original understandings, they condensed the 12 Steps of Anonymous programs back down to 8 Principles or Choices coupled with Bible references. Since then millions more have followed their highly-successful Celebrate Recovery® (CR) program to find freedom in Christ and victory over a wide array of common human difficulties.

Over the years, many have observed that Step programs capture the essential and lifelong Biblical dynamics involved in becoming a spiritually born again believer and active disciple of Jesus Christ. 12-Step programs may hold meetings in houses of worship but choose to operate independently of religion. On the other hand, CR was designed to be sponsored by local churches as an outreach ministry with a focus on people who self-identify as needing recovery from a number of challenging life situations, including addictions. In any given area there also may or may not be an active CR presence, a situation that calls for

**Background Material**

a discipleship program with a wider reach and deeper integration with the core mission of the church.

Sadly, struggles with pornography and other negative or destructive attitudes or behaviors that impair a Christian's walk with Christ are not generally covered in pulpit messages or new member classes for a number of reasons. Perhaps it's because people may be reluctant to be open about potentially embarrassing problems or individual home fellowship groups or congregations may lack the capacity to handle them. Access to Christian growth and discipleship resources for helping members and new believers overcome personal issues and become solidly rooted in their faith may also be limited.

Now in the 21$^{st}$ century we are again facing widespread social changes that are challenging the moral and spiritual roots of our civilization. As the prophet said,

*Justice is turned back, and righteousness stands far away; for truth has stumbled in the public squares, and uprightness cannot enter.* Isaiah 59:14

Many of us find ourselves aching for an outpouring of God's Holy Spirit, for times of widespread revival and spiritual awakening. Are we prepared? What would happen if God were to answer our prayers and pour out His Spirit throughout our communities, breaking open those already in the church and bringing in a large influx of new believers laden with the issues of our modern world? Would we and our churches know how to handle an Awakening like this?

Celebrate Salvation® has taken the Oxford Group's understandings, as modified by 12-Step and CR programs, and clarified them further with grateful credit to make them available to the church at large.

Discovering the ever-unfolding mystery of faith in the living God is a wonderfully profound, life-changing, and satisfying gift. Our hope is that this modest series of introductory studies will provide a Biblically balanced and sound foundation for the faith which is widely applicable, reproducible, and fruitful. Please use the materials in *The Joy of Christian Discipleship Series* and augment them with those of your own fellowship group as we seek to meet the needs of our time with God's faithful Word.

> *Dr. Bill Morehouse*
> October 2020

**Meeting 21$^{st}$ Century Needs**

# Celebrate Salvation!®
## *The Joy of Christian Discipleship Course 1*
### Established in 3 Stages and 7 Steps

## Saved! Rescued by Grace
### A – Foundational Principles of the Good News

1. **Recognize the trouble I'm in:** Admit that I'm dealing with issues that are beyond my control and need help getting and keeping my life on the right track.

2. **Believe in God's love:** Believe that God is really in charge, loves me, and earnestly desires to exercise His Kingdom power to rescue me and work it all out.

3. **Let go and let God:** Consciously choose to commit all my life and will to Jesus Christ's care and control.

## Sanctified: Coming Clean with God
### B – Living in the Word and the World

4. **Conviction and Repentance:** Evaluate my life and all my relationships in the light of the Holy Spirit and then openly confess my faults to myself, to God, and to others that I trust. Forgive those who have hurt me and seek restitution and reconciliation wherever possible.

5. **Trust and Obey:** Voluntarily submit to any and all changes God wants to make in my life and humbly ask Him to cleanse me and progressively remove all my character defects.

6. **Communicating with God:** Reserve dedicated time with God for self-examination, Bible reading, fasting and prayer in order to know God and His will for my life and to gain the power to follow His will.

## Sent: Becoming a Living Letter
### C – Sharing the Good News of God's Kingdom

7. **The Great Commission:** Celebrate the joy of my salvation by following God's lead in bringing His Good News to others in word, deed, and power.

**Background Material**

# About Course 1

The material in **Course 1** of *The Joy of Christian Discipleship Series* has been developed in the form of three books, 1-3, one for each foundational Stage of Christian discipleship with significant expansion on the Great Commission in the third. These workbooks are designed to serve as study guides for small discipleship groups of 2-12 (ideal 3-8 committed) members. Each of the three studies can be completed in about 12 weekly group sessions over one semester or 3-month period with breaks for holidays.

New groups may gather and start at any time with mature leaders who have already gone through the material themselves or have been raised up in similar 12-Step and/or CR programs in other settings. A good way for congregations to get a Celebrate Salvation® course going in their church is to gather current members together who have had some experience in discipleship or recovery groups and embark on a planning process for reviewing and introducing the study series into the life of their fellowship. It's not only wise but essential to plan on organizing separate groups for men and women, given the personal nature of discipleship and the relationships that develop, including those between leaders and members newer in the faith.

Each of the three guides in **Course 1** is divided into twelve 4-page weekly lessons containing four lessons on each of the three Steps in the first two guides and four lessons on carrying out the Great Commission in Word, Deed, and Power in the third. Supplementary handouts and worksheets designed to accompany each book in the series are available in a companion book or online at www.celebratesalvation.org/more).

This second guide is entitled *"Sanctified: Coming Clean with God"* and covers what it means to cooperate with your LORD and Savior in cleansing and rebuilding your life on His firm foundation so that you can live in the world in accordance with Paul's instructions to Timothy:

> *Therefore, if anyone cleanses himself from what is dishonorable, he will be a vessel for honorable use, set apart as holy, useful to the master of the house, ready for every good work.*
> 2 Timothy 2:21

Or, as Pastor Bob Mumford once quipped, "Jesus loves you just the way you are, but He doesn't want to leave you that way."

**Discipleship Course Design**

# Group Guidelines

1. Prepare for each meeting by reading the week's lesson and writing out your answers to the questions in advance.
2. Try to keep your group sharing focused on your own thoughts, feelings, experiences, and insights about each question. Limit your sharing to 3 minutes.
3. There is NO cross-talk. Cross-talk is when two people engage in side conversations during the meeting that exclude others. Each person is free to express their own feelings without interruptions.
4. We are here to support one another, not to instruct, preach at, or "fix" one another.
5. Anonymity and confidentiality are essential requirements in a trusting discipleship group. Personal information that is shared in the group stays in the group. The only exception is when someone threatens to injure themselves or others.
6. Offensive or demeaning language has no place in a Christian fellowship group.
7. Please silence your personal electronic devices and put them away. Recording during meetings is prohibited.

## Suggestions for Group Leadership

Organize separate groups for men and women to ensure safe, open sharing. Schedule regular weekly meetings to last about 90 minutes. Make sure all participants have study guides. Find out who needs help with handouts.

+ Gather group in a circle and open meeting on time with prayer and brief comments about group business and upcoming events.
+ Go around circle with introductions including first name, brief confession of faith, and primary issues for personal growth.
+ Continue around circle by reading 3 Stages and 7 Steps, followed by Guidelines and then, as a group, one of the Confessional Prayers.
+ Start each lesson by reading the introductory paragraphs around the circle and then opening with the first question.
+ Keep one-by-one sharing going around the circle within Guidelines.
+ Circulate basket for prayer requests; then recirculate so each person who submitted one can take a different one home for intercession.
+ Bring copies of next week's handouts to pass out to those who need them.
+ Close meeting on time with prayer, allowing members to linger for conversation for a while. Refreshments optional.

## Background Material

# Confession and Prayer

## The 23rd Psalm

*The LORD is my shepherd; I shall not want. He makes me lie down in green pastures. He leads me beside still waters. He restores my soul. He leads me in paths of righteousness for his name's sake. Even though I walk through the valley of the shadow of death, I will fear no evil, for you are with me; your rod and your staff, they comfort me. You prepare a table before me in the presence of my enemies; you anoint my head with oil; my cup overflows. Surely goodness and mercy shall follow me all the days of my life, and I shall dwell in the house of the LORD forever.*

**David**

## The LORD's Prayer

*"Our Father in heaven, hallowed be Your Name. Your Kingdom come, Your will be done on earth as it is in heaven. Give us this day our daily bread, and forgive us our debts, as we forgive our debtors. Do not lead us into temptation, but deliver us from the evil one, for Yours is the Kingdom and the power and the glory forever. Amen."*

**Jesus**

## The Serenity Prayer

*God, grant me the serenity to accept the things I cannot change, the courage to change the things I can, and the wisdom to know the difference. Living one day at a time, enjoying one moment at a time; accepting hardship as a pathway to peace; taking, as Jesus did, this sinful world as it is, not as I would have it; trusting that You will make all things right if I surrender to Your will; so that I may be reasonably happy in this life and supremely happy with You forever in the next. Amen.*

**Reinhold Niebuhr**

# A New Operating System

Becoming a Christian is more than learning new ways of handling life: it's a whole new way of living. As the Apostle Paul wrote:

*Therefore, if anyone is in Christ, he is a new creation. The old has passed away; behold, the new has come.*
                                                              2 Corinthians 5:17

Jesus described the process to Nicodemus, a prominent leader in the Jewish Senate (Sanhedrin) at the time, in these words:

*This man came to Jesus by night and said to him, "Rabbi, we know that you are a teacher come from God, for no one can do these signs that you do unless God is with him." Jesus answered him, "Truly, truly, I say to you, unless one is born again he cannot see the kingdom of God." Nicodemus said to him, "How can a man be born when he is old? Can he enter a second time into his mother's womb and be born?" Jesus answered, "Truly, truly, I say to you, unless one is born of water and the Spirit, he cannot enter the kingdom of God. That which is born of the flesh is flesh, and that which is born of the Spirit is spirit. Do not marvel that I said to you, 'You must be born again.' The wind blows where it wishes, and you hear its sound, but you do not know where it comes from or where it goes. So it is with everyone who is born of the Spirit."*
                                                              John 3:2-8

In today's world a helpful way to look at what happens when a person becomes a converted believer in Jesus is to compare our situation with that of a modern computer. Just as baby is born with an intricate brain preprogrammed to handle the basic instincts of human life and then grows, learns, and adds new programs and data, a computer comes from the factory with an electronic central processing unit (CPU) and a basic operating system (OS) like Apple or Windows, along with capacity for programs and memory. As the computer is used, more programs and data are added.

However, computers can and do get corrupted over time like the human beings who own them. Bad programs and malware get installed, either intentionally or unwittingly. Data is accumulated in memory that may be corrupt to begin with or actually corrupted by the invasion of computer viruses. As people we try to clean up our acts and reform our ways to varying degrees. This is like tidying up our computers,

**Background Material**

eliminating programs and files, and running antivirus scans to remove malware. These are good ideas, but our underlying operating systems remain the same. Nothing is really new.

What if we could go beyond cleaning up and rebooting our lives, so to speak, and actually start over again with a different operating system entirely? Well, in Christ we not only can but that's actually what we're called to do as spiritually "born again" believers. If and when we turn ourselves completely over to Him, He takes over, installs an amazing new Kingdom operating system (no bite out of this apple) in the very heart of our being, and attaches us to a new source of power.

He then enlists our cooperation in submitting to being scanned for malware, including incompatible worldview *"-isms"* like *"racism"* etc. (see handout called **What is an** *"-ism"*?). After the Holy Spirit guides us through a thorough inventory, the LORD sorts out, cleans up, and reinstalls some programs and data we need from our old setup. Some of it, but not everything. Did you make excuses for breaking the 10 Commandments? Were you a sex worker? Were you a heavy drinker? Did you cheat at work or on your taxes? Did you reject the Bible and throw Jesus out with the bath? Skip those programs and redeem that data: He has better ones to replace them.

When you've converted over entirely and have taken time to learn the new system and add personal material from your studies, you'll find that it has an amazing new power supply and works much better than the old. You won't long for the leeks and quails of Egypt anymore and will learn to enjoy and appreciate receiving God's provision on the way to the Promised Land. And once you've settled into your "new normal" as a believer, you'll discover that you have peace and joy and power that you never knew before.

Through new birth we receive not only eternal life in Christ (as if that were not enough) but an entirely new life guided and empowered by His Holy Spirit to live fruitfully and joyfully in the here and now. It's a job worth humbly investing the dedication and time to do well.

**A New Operating System**

# Sanctified: Coming Clean with God
## Living in the Word and the World

*We have all become like one who is unclean, and all our righteous deeds are like a polluted garment.*

Isaiah 64:6

*Therefore, if anyone cleanses himself from what is dishonorable, he will be a vessel for honorable use, set apart as holy, useful to the master of the house, ready for every good work.*

2 Timothy 2:21

*Christ loved the church* [ekklesia] *and gave himself up for her, that he might sanctify her, having cleansed her by the washing of water with the Word, so that he might present the church to himself in splendor, without spot or wrinkle or any such thing, that she might be holy and without blemish.*

Ephesians 5:25-27

*Beloved, we are God's children now, and what we will be has not yet appeared; but we know that when he appears we shall be like him, because we shall see him as he is. And everyone who thus hopes in him purifies himself as he is pure.*

1 John 3:2-3

*Now may the God of peace himself sanctify you completely, and may your whole spirit and soul and body be kept blameless at the coming of our* LORD *Jesus Christ. He who calls you is faithful; he will surely do it.*

1 Thessalonians 5:23-24

To understand what's going on here, we need to look at things from God's point of view. From our point of view we might be in pretty good shape and just need some touching up to make us really useful in His Kingdom. Or we might think we're such basket cases that not even God could find any use for us.

Actually, we're more mixed up than we can even imagine, but God loves us, sees the good in us, and has chosen to call us aside for some major restoration so that we can enjoy life, love others, and find our place in His Kingdom on this fallen earth.

Some of what needs to be dealt with is obvious in our external appearance and behavior. Other disorders are more hidden, subtle, and pervasive and have to do with our underlying attitudes, feelings,

10

motivations, prejudices, and orientation to God, life, others, and the world in general.

According to the Operator's Manual, we need a good inspection, scrubbing, and restoration inside and out, as well as an everlasting power supply and ongoing service. However, along the way we still need to keep on living, relating, and working in the world. How on earth will this happen? Actually, it's all part of the proper functioning of our new operating system. With God all things are possible! All we need to do is yield and cooperate with Him.

Jesus said this about the soul-searching work of the Holy Spirit in John 16:8, *"And when he comes, he will convict the world concerning sin and righteousness and judgment."* When a person comes to Christ, they become acutely aware of their own faults (sin) in comparison with Christ's beauty and sacrificial service (righteousness). Usually the worst and most current failings become visible right away.

As time goes on, more and more evidences of sin rise from their buried places in our hearts into consciousness. The natural tendency is to push them back down, cover them up again, and harden our hearts to keep them down. We defend, deny, rationalize and hide, hoping our soiled conscience will settle again.

What we're about to do during this study is quite the opposite: we're going to dive in and cooperate with the Holy Spirit in making a thorough personal inventory of our lives, uncovering both the good and bad and inviting Him to purify, restore, strengthen, and establish us in the joyful love and fruit of His Kingdom.

Fear not! Every flaw that you discover together is one more that you can cooperate with Him in eliminating from your future and replacing with His more perfect way of doing things.

*For by a single offering he has perfected for all time those who are being sanctified.*

Hebrews 10:14

*He knows the way that I take; when he has tried me, I shall come out as gold.*

Job 23:10

**Living in the Word and the World**

# Lesson 1B
# Taking a Personal Inventory

**Step 4: Conviction and Repentance:** Evaluate my life and all my relationships in the light of the Holy Spirit and then openly confess my faults to myself, to God, and to others that I trust. Forgive those who have hurt me and seek restitution and reconciliation wherever possible.

Meet with the Great Physician and Wonderful Counselor and allow the Holy Spirit to guide me in doing a Complete Personal Inventory that includes both strengths and weaknesses.

---

*Search me, O God, and know my heart! Try me and know my thoughts! And see if there be any grievous way in me, and lead me in the way everlasting!*

Psalm 139:23-24

This is where we begin to evaluate the strengths and weaknesses of our upbringing and life experiences, including examining the origins of the personal hurts, disappointments, anger, low-self-esteem, defensiveness, and other bad baggage that have estranged us from God and strained or broken our relationship with Him and others.

Our Complete Personal Inventory covers a lot of territory. We want to set aside time to revisit our lives to see how we got to where we are. What happened to us as we were growing up? How did we react? Where did we go off the path? Where was our heavenly Father in our story? How were we hurt? What troublesome hang-ups and habits did we get? Who do we trust?

Then we want to look at the way things have played out in our lives. What have we done with the God of the universe who created us and loved us so much that He sent His only begotten Son to save us and His Holy Spirit to encourage and guide us? How are we taking care of what we've been given? Have we related to the people around us with integrity, love, and respect? Are we good stewards of our bodies, talents, time and treasure? What are our priorities?

**Sanctified: Coming Clean With God**

As you start the Inventory process, please remember:

1.  Everyone has strengths and weaknesses, and you are somewhere in the middle of the pack. So don't think too highly or too poorly of yourself – keep it balanced.

2.  There are two kinds of mistakes people make: errors of "omission" or things we don't do that we should and errors of "commission" or doing things wrong. You and the people and institutions around you have made both kinds – be gentle, kind, and forgiving. Let go, and let God. The past has gone by, and all we can do is allow Him to clean up the mess and change the future.

*Whoever conceals his transgressions will not prosper, but he who confesses and forsakes them will obtain mercy.*                    Proverbs 28:13

A good place to start is by inviting the Holy Spirit to guide your thoughts and meditations as you go through and then write down your recollections, both positive and negative, starting with our **Life Survey Worksheet** available online at www.celebratesalvation.org/more. If there is generational privilege or trauma in your family's history, you may wish to review and fill out our **Family History Worksheet** also.

Will taking a Complete Personal Inventory be an uncomfortable process? Yes, it might be for a while, but take comfort in God's Word:

*After you have suffered a little while, the God of all grace, who has called you to his eternal glory in Christ, will himself restore, confirm, strengthen, and establish you.*

1 Peter 5:3

## Personal Life Survey

1.  Who were the significant people in your early life up through Grade School and what happened that had an impact on you?

2. What were the significant events or developments, positive and negative, during your adolescence through High School?

3. What impacted your life after you went to college and/or started your career, marriage or family?

4. Did problems arise or develop later in your middle years or beyond?

5. Wherever you are in life, even if you've passed through all of these stages, what problems are you still working on?

Be particularly thorough in each area of your Life Survey by taking additional notes on the Worksheets and in your journal. This is a time when it's especially important to develop a trustworthy relationship with an accountability partner and committing or recommitting to maintaining a daily journal.

## Memorizing Scripture

Another excellent spiritual discipline to develop as you grow as a disciple is memorizing Scripture. Notice that we've suggested a number of short Scripture passages for memorization in the Study Guides by printing them in dark blue. Each one is pertinent to the lessons being covered.

This Lesson started with a suggested passage from Psalm 139 and ends with two more below. It always helps to understand the context of what you're committing to memory, so try to look up each passage and read the verses that precede and follow it, then repeat the passage several times to capture it in your memory bank. Repeat it again for review later on, and it will be yours!

*All Scripture is breathed out by God and profitable for teaching, for reproof, for correction, and for training in righteousness,* 2 Timothy 3:16

*"It is written, 'Man shall not live by bread alone, but by every word that comes from the mouth of God.'"* Matthew 4:4 (**from** Deuteronomy 8:3)

# Lesson 2B
# Alienation from God

**Step 4: Conviction and Repentance:** Evaluate my life and all my relationships in the light of the Holy Spirit and then openly confess my faults to myself, to God, and to others that I trust. Forgive those who have hurt me and seek restitution and reconciliation wherever possible.

Spirit (Greek *pneumo*): Evaluate factors influencing spiritual estrangement and alienation from God including offense, pride, arrogance, and self-will. Discover and work toward developing godly humility and yieldedness.

---

Human beings are intimately woven together in three parts – spirit, soul, and body – and we can have problems in all three. In the upcoming lessons we'll be covering each area, starting with our spiritual life, the part of us that was truly made in God's image.

Almost all our problems can be traced to one tap root: we've lost our conscious connection with our Creator and put our trust in ourselves, in others, and in our possessions instead.

How did that happen? We each have our own stories. Perhaps we never heard about the presence and fatherly love of the living God and just took the beauty of creation and goodness around us for granted. Or we went to church and found a form of religion that had no power. Maybe we had our hopes up and were so disappointed or offended by things we've experienced as we were growing up that we left God behind. There are many distractions and false detours along the way that can lead us astray also. In the final analysis, however, it's our own "sin" (error) added to that of others that separates and seals us off from God.

Taking pride in our God-given talents and gifts without giving credit to the source, rejecting our upbringing and going our own way, and pursuing false goals and gods takes its toll. We may even have become ensnared in occult or addictive behaviors that cry out for identification, renunciation, and appealing to God for cleansing and restoration.

**Sanctified: Coming Clean With God**

During this study we will be inviting the Holy Spirit to search our hearts for spiritual damage and reveal the negative effects our spiritual alienation has had on our behavior and character development. Only then can we be empowered to seek God for forgiveness, healing, reconciliation, and adoption as newborn children into His family.

How can we best approach this? The simple answer is with humility:

*But he gives more grace. Therefore it says, "God opposes the proud but gives grace to the humble."*

James 4:6

*The sacrifices of God are a broken spirit; a broken and contrite heart, O God, you will not despise.*

Psalm 51:17

*But to all who did receive him, who believed in his name, he gave the right to become children of God, who were born, not of blood nor of the will of the flesh nor of the will of man, but of God.*

John 1:12, 13

Set aside some quality time when you can be alone with God. Have your journal or a pad of paper and pen at hand and spend some focused time in prayer, meditation, and reflection on your life experiences with God and faith up until now.

We've developed a **Spiritual Life Worksheet** (available online at www.celebratesalvation.org/more) that you may also print out and use as an interactive guide to prompt you as you prepare to respond to the questions below.

## Spiritual Life Survey

1.  How do you view brokenness, as a strength or a weakness? How did you learn to deal with feeling broken?

2. When did you first hear about or become aware of God? How did you and your family handle that?

3. Was there a time when you committed your life to Christ and what happened afterwards?

4. Have you had problems believing and placing your trust (faith) in God as your heavenly Father? If so, what are they and why?

5.  Have any other religious or occult beliefs or practices influenced your ideas about the reality and nature of God?

6.  What part, if any, has church participation or ministry had in your life? Has it alienated you or drawn you closer?

Be thorough in each area of your Spiritual Life Survey by taking additional notes on the Worksheets, below, and/or in a separate pad. Seriously consider committing or recommitting to maintaining a daily Journal of your insights, meditations, prayers, and thoughts. This is also a time when it's especially important to start developing a trustworthy relationship with an accountability partner.

# Lesson 3B
# Human relationships

**Step 4: Conviction and Repentance:** Evaluate my life and all my relationships in the light of the Holy Spirit and then openly confess my faults to myself, to God, and to others that I trust. Forgive those who have hurt me and seek restitution and reconciliation wherever possible.

Soul (Greek *psyche*): Evaluate my upbringing and life experiences for insights about my psychological health and human relationships.

---

*We know that for those who love God all things work together for good, for those who are called according to his purpose.*
Romans 8:28

In 12-Step programs, the evaluation we are calling a "Complete Personal Inventory" is described as "a fearless moral inventory." The word moral means "concerned with the principles of right and wrong behavior and the goodness or badness of human character" and has to do with not only what we are doing or have done that is right or wrong but with how our character developed.

Why is God interested in the details of my past? Can't we just draw a line now and leave the messy past behind in forgetfulness, as some claim that Paul's confession to the Philippians means:

*But one thing I do: forgetting what lies behind and straining forward to what lies ahead, I press on toward the goal for the prize of the upward call of God in Christ Jesus.*
Philippians 3:13-14

Like all other portions of Scripture, this passage is understood best in the context of the verses that surround it. As we mature in our faith we certainly aren't to dwell on and live in the past, but it's difficult to choose to forget things that you haven't examined and been prepared by God to move beyond, as revealed in the following quote:

**Sanctified: Coming Clean With God**

*"The present is always haunted by the things that have happened in childhood. Often, we think we are so grown up and we've left our childhood feelings behind, but that isn't true. The things that hurt us remain the same, and they hurt us even more as adults because we've held on to them for a long time."*

Souvankham Thammavongsa – *The Inner Lives of Children*

Don't be surprised if you discover ingrained negative attitudes of prejudice against whole groups of people. We've already encountered the foundational difficulty we face with the mistakes and damage of our past: we can't fix our own problems. All we can do is recognize them, turn them over to God, and let Him guide us with His grace and mercy through the healing and restoration process.

*If we confess our sins, he is faithful and just and will forgive us our sins and purify us from all unrighteousness.*          1 John 1:9

Once we've come to grips with our past behaviors and issues, we'll discover that timely confession, giving and receiving forgiveness, turning people and relationships over to God, and making amends where that's called for is the ongoing solution. Some hurts and amends can be worked out interpersonally, but there are others that are better handled between you, God, and trusted confidants only.

Use the **Interpersonal Worksheets**, both **Helps** and **Hurts** (available at www.celebratesalvation.org/more), as interactive guides to prompt you as you respond to the questions below:

## Interpersonal Life Survey

1.  Who have you hurt with your wrong attitudes, words and actions? Make a list, starting with the most recent.

2.  Who has hurt you, currently and in the past, and how have you handled it? Don't forget old issues with family members.

3.  Are there any people or groups that you've wronged or been wronged by that need more than confession and repentance?

4.  Have you developed pride, anger, resentments, estrangement, or other destructive ways of handling your relationship issues?

5.  Do you still have negative attitudes or symptoms like fear or avoidance from what you or others have done?

6.  How have people let God's grace shine through and helped you grow? (Note: people's good deeds don't balance, excuse, or overcome any hurtful things they may have done.)

Be thorough in each area of your Interpersonal Life Survey by taking additional notes on the Worksheets and/or in a separate pad. Seriously consider deepening your commitment to maintaining a daily Journal of your insights, meditations, prayers, and thoughts. Remember: This is the time to start developing a trustworthy relationship with an accountability partner.

# Lesson 4B
# Godly stewardship

**Step 4: Conviction and Repentance:** Evaluate my life and all my relationships in the light of the Holy Spirit and then openly confess my faults to myself, to God, and to others that I trust. Forgive those who have hurt me and seek restitution and reconciliation wherever possible.

Body (Greek *soma*): Evaluate the way I manage my physical well-being, including dysfunctional practices and habits with nutrition, hygiene, exercise, sexuality, possessions, and the environment I live in.

---

*'All things are lawful for me,' but not all things are helpful. 'All things are lawful for me,' but I will not be dominated by anything. 'Food is meant for the stomach and the stomach for food' – and God will destroy both one and the other. The body is not meant for sexual immorality, but for the LORD, and the LORD for the body… Or do you not know that your body is a temple of the Holy Spirit within you, whom you have from God? You are not your own, for you were bought with a price. So glorify God in your body.*

1 Corinthians 6:12-13, 19-20

How are we taking care of our physical bodies and their needs? Are we being good stewards of what has been entrusted to us? Are we respecting balance and boundaries and glorifying God in our bodies? Let's divide our evaluation into the five main dimensions of our physical lives: food, hygiene and exercise, sexuality, shelter, and our environment (nature, air and water).

Many of us find that our emotions become entangled with what we do with our bodies. We seek comfort in food and drink, sexual activities and possessions, repetitive behaviors, bad habits, and even addictions. How are you doing with maintaining a balanced diet, what you're eating as well as how much and when? Do you depend on food or substances for anxiety control or comfort?

**Sanctified: Coming Clean With God**

Have you gotten out of shape by avoiding regular activity or do you exercise so much that you rely on the release it gives you?

Are you managing your sexuality and its expression within God's will? The Bible has a lot to say about sex because it can be such a big problem area for so many of us. Think about the self-centered consequences of wandering eyes, lust, masturbation, adultery, fornication, pornography, and all the so-called "crimes without victims" that drag so many people down into the dirt with self-justification and self-loathing. Come clean with God, yourself, and trustworthy accountability partners in this critical area of life.

What about your shelter, houses and clothing, and the belongings that you surround yourself with? Are you jealous of what other people have or ungrateful for what God has given you? Do you appreciate and take good care of your possessions? Do you respect other people's property? Do you want things so badly that you will steal to get them?

Finally, how are you demonstrating your care for our shared environment? To stimulate thought you might want to print out and use the **Stewardship Worksheet** as an interactive guide (available online at www.celebratesalvation.org/more) as you respond to these queries and the questions below:

## Stewardship Survey

1. Are you overweight, a binge eater, anorectic, or too concerned about food? Do you rely on smoking, drugs, or alcohol?

2.  Do you have problems with sexual fantasies or activity outside of the boundaries of marriage? Are you hooked on the Internet?

3.  What about your physical activity and fitness? Have you made improvement plans only to break them again?

4.  How much of your identity is in what you own or have? Are you a good steward of your time, money, and possessions?

5. Do you pay any attention to concerns about the quality of our natural resources like air and water or just leave it to others?

Be thorough while you're at it by taking additional notes in each area of your Stewardship Survey below, on the Worksheets, and/or in a separate pad. Endeavor to solidify your commitment to maintaining a daily Journal of your insights, meditations, prayers, and thoughts as well as sharing with your accountability partner. And don't forget to try memorizing some Scriptures!

# Lesson 5B
# A personal relationship

**Step 5: Trust and Obey:** Voluntarily submit to any and all changes God wants to make in my life and humbly ask Him to cleanse me and progressively remove all my character defects.

Seek and develop an ongoing personal relationship of love, friendship, and mutual understanding with the living God.

---

The triune God who called us into being already understands everything about us from beginning to end. This is a challenging idea for our minds to grasp, since God is infinite in His understanding and dwells both within and beyond the time and space He created. He is the God of the universe, the awesome Creator, Sustainer, and LORD of all.

*Where were you when I laid the foundation of the earth? Tell me, if you have understanding. Who determined its measurements — surely you know! Or who stretched the line upon it? On what were its bases sunk, or who laid its cornerstone, when the morning stars sang together and all the sons of God shouted for joy?*
Job 38:4-7

How on earth can we have a personal relationship with such an overwhelming God? It is only because His love for us is as profound and all-encompassing as He is Himself. God took the initiative:

*For God so loved the world that he gave his only Son, that whoever believes in him should not perish but have eternal life. For God did not send his Son into the world to condemn the world, but in order that the world might be saved through him.*
John 3:16-17

*"Behold, I stand at the door and knock. If anyone hears my voice and opens the door, I will come in to him and eat with him, and he with me."*
Revelation 3:20

How can we resist a God who has had good plans for us since before the foundations of the earth? Well, the fact of the matter is that we all have problems. First we have to believe that what is revealed about Him in the Bible is true, then let it sink in, and finally learn to trust that

**Sanctified: Coming Clean With God**

He can communicate with us in the here and now even though we can't see Him physically.

*"Blessed are those who have not seen and yet have believed."* John 20:29

For us to develop a mutual understanding involves learning about and receiving God's understanding of who we are and who He is so that we can take my rightful places, reciprocate, and benefit mutually from a growing relationship with Him as our heavenly Father through Jesus, our Savior and LORD.

The process involves trusting Him enough to put aside any other priorities, "gods" (idols), or personal aspirations that we hold alongside or place above Him and His plans for our lives and then opening our hearts to Him in prayer. When we share our inmost secrets, thoughts, and yearnings with our heavenly Father in prayer, we affirm that we know what He already knows about us and open ourselves up to receive His forgiveness, guidance, and wisdom.

*If any of you lacks wisdom, let him ask God, who gives generously to all without reproach, and it will be given him.* James 1:5

As you prepare to consider how yielded you are to God, consider rereading Romans 7 and 8, focusing on the passage quoted after the questions at the end of this lesson.

## My Yieldedness to God

1. What obstacles do you see to being adopted by and developing a personal relationship with God as your Father?

2. Have you begun having a regular time of devotions and prayer? How is it going so far?

3. Has your conscience been quickened to prompt you when you are straying from godly boundaries and behavior?

4. Do you struggle with feeling condemned by God? Is guilt or shame blocking your freedom in prayer?

5.  How can you add gratitude and thanksgiving to your personal time with God to balance the weight of some of your petitions?

Reflect on the following passage from Romans 8 while you're responding to each question and take notes below as well as on additional sheets of paper or in an ongoing daily journal of your insights, meditations, prayers, and thoughts. Share with your accountability partner along the way.

*For I consider that the sufferings of this present time are not worth comparing with the glory that is to be revealed to us. For the creation waits with eager longing for the revealing of the sons of God. For the creation was subjected to futility, not willingly, but because of him who subjected it, in hope that the creation itself will be set free from its bondage to corruption and obtain the freedom of the glory of the children of God. For we know that the whole creation has been groaning together in the pains of childbirth until now. And not only the creation, but we ourselves, who have the firstfruits of the Spirit, groan inwardly as we wait eagerly for adoption as sons, the redemption of our bodies.* Romans 8:18-23

# Lesson 6B
## Accountability

**Step 5: Trust and Obey:** Voluntarily submit to any and all changes God wants to make in my life and humbly ask Him to cleanse me and progressively remove all my character defects.

Developing mutual relationships of accountability with a seasoned advocate and knowledgeable partners of the same sex. How to bypass triggers and seek support to prevent or recover quickly from mental or behavioral relapses.

---

*Trust in the LORD with all your heart, and do not lean on your own understanding. In all your ways acknowledge him, and he will make straight your paths.*                    Proverbs 3:5-6

Business leaders have discovered that accountability is the single biggest differentiator between successful and unsuccessful enterprises. The same is actually true in each of our lives. If someone isn't accountable to anyone beyond themselves, they can end up becoming what people call a "no-account" who takes credit for their successes and blames their failures on outside factors.

We've discovered that relying on ourselves instead of God leads to error, disappointment, and failure. In addition to being accountable to Him, God asks us to be humble and take counsel from the Word of God, from Him directly in prayer, and from trustworthy people around us.

He urges us to listen and be obedient to all of the authorities He has put over us for the common good and our protection, including those in our extended families, church, workplace, study group, and community. This is what it means to be "meek" – not mousey or weak but finding our places of responsibility in each area of our lives and filling them with dedication and diligence.

*Obey your leaders and submit to them, for they are keeping watch over your souls, as those who will have to give an account. Let them do this with joy and not with groaning, for that would be of no advantage to you.*   Hebrews 1:17

**Sanctified: Coming Clean With God**

As we go through the steps in our discipleship study, we're all urged to seek guidance from a knowledgeable mentor or advocate who knows us and the content of the material we're going through. Sometimes we need a knowledgeable, mature believer to lean on when we get confused about what's happening in our lives or in the group. We'll also be relying on the mutual support we receive from each other as well as developing an ongoing relationship with at least one trustworthy accountability partner that we can connect and get together with regularly to share and pray.

*And let us consider how to stir up one another to love and good works.*

Hebrews 10:24

We've been through the preliminary process of taking a complete inventory. Just as repentance isn't a one-time event but an integral part of a disciple's lifestyle, so is remaining open to conviction, self-examination, and ongoing sanctification. As you grow in your faith you may wish to use our **Periodic Review Worksheet** (accessible at www.celebratesalvation.org/more) to review your progress.

## My Accountability

1.  Do you think you're growing in your ability to share openly with God, receive His love and forgiveness, and seek His wisdom? List some examples.

2. How have you related to authority in the past, especially to the authority of a father, employer, or community officer?

3. Do you have trouble sharing personally with other people about areas of difficulty in your life?

4. Have you ever received counseling? If so, were you able to receive and profit from the input you were given?

5.  Have you identified an advocate and an accountability partner that you can share with about the issues raised by this study?

Be thorough while you're answering each question by taking notes below as well as on additional sheets of paper or in an ongoing daily journal of your insights, meditations, prayers, and thoughts. Don't forget to share with your accountability partner and try memorizing some Scriptures!

# Lesson 7B
# Discerning the will of God

**Step 5: Trust and Obey:** Voluntarily submit to any and all changes God wants to make in my life and humbly ask Him to cleanse me and progressively remove all my character defects.

Learn to discern God's voice of guidance clearly through comparing my thoughts with the Word of God, confirming with an inner witness and providential circumstances, and checking with mature believers.

---

We've just spent some time investigating accountability, which is a major element in God's plan for revealing His Kingdom in our lives and surroundings. "When is the Kingdom of God coming?" Jesus was asked by some Pharisees while He was out teaching. His response indicated that the Kingdom was already there:

> *"The kingdom of God is not coming in ways that can be observed, nor will they say, 'Look, here it is!' or 'There!' for behold, the kingdom of God is in the midst of you."*
> Luke 17:20-21

First, let's take a look at what this "Kingdom of God" might be. Very simply God's Kingdom is the realm where He is in charge and things go the way He would like them to. This Kingdom encompasses the entire natural universe with one exception: Man has free will and can choose in any given moment whether or not to be yielded to his Creator's guidance. Everything else is guided by God's laws, but Man may choose to be an outlaw.

Therefore, we are surrounded by God's Kingdom, as suggested by the modern translation above, However, we are invited and may choose to allow Him full reign within us as well, as indicated by translating the Greek word ἐντὸς (*entos*) more accurately as "within" rather than "in the midst of" you. What this indicates is that we have been given the ability within our thought life to discern God's will as revealed by the Holy Spirit as well as the choice to obey or disobey it. But how?

**Sanctified: Coming Clean With God**

*"Ask, and it will be given to you; seek, and you will find; knock, and it will be opened to you" ... If any of you lacks wisdom, let him ask God, who gives generously to all without reproach, and it will be given him.*

Matthew 7:7 and James 1:5

If we are earnest in our asking, seeking, and knocking, God's inner guidance is readily accessible. However, it's always good to seek confirmation, especially while we're learning discernment and when serious decisions are being made. There are four tests that should line up for inner guidance to be confirmed, tests which become automatic with practice:

1. Does Gods' written Word in the Bible agree or disagree?

2. Do you have an inner witness from your indwelling Savior that you're on the right track?

3. Do mature fellow believers share your inner witness?

4. Do your current circumstances appear to confirm it?

Ideally, all four should agree, especially the first one, which makes learning the Word of God by heart so vital. With ongoing practice believers can learn to access moment-by-moment guidance confidently for even the simplest things in life.

## My Discernment

1. Have you had experience with God's inner "voice" of loving protection and guidance? How have you handled it?

2. Can you think of any times when you didn't heed the warnings of your conscience? What happened?

3. Have you been receiving encouragement and guidance from God recently? Note some examples.

4. Confessing that God in Christ is not only your Savior but your LORD makes you accountable to Him. How are you doing?

5.  What questions do you have about discerning God's will in your life? Have you asked your pastor or advocate about them?

Be thorough while you're answering each question by taking notes below as well as on additional sheets of paper or in an ongoing daily journal of your insights, meditations, prayers, and thoughts. Don't forget to share with your accountability partner and try memorizing some Scriptures!

# Lesson 8B
# The Great Commandment

**Step 5: Trust and Obey:** Voluntarily submit to any and all changes God wants to make in my life and humbly ask Him to cleanse me and progressively remove all my character defects.

Make love your aim. Identify and seek God's help in overcoming any prejudices, racial or cultural, and lack of trust stemming from fear, negative experiences, or distorted upbringing.

---

*And* [Jesus] *said to him, "You shall love the* LORD *your God with all your heart and with all your soul and with all your mind. This is the great and* **first** *commandment.*

*And a* **second** [The Golden Rule] *is like it: You shall love your neighbor as yourself. On these two commandments depend all the Law and the Prophets."*

Matthew 22:37-40

Jesus summarized the instruction of the entire Old Testament in these two statements. The first is essentially a rephrasing and expansion of the first of the Ten Commandments given to Moses

*You shall have no other gods before me.* Exodus 20:3

while the second summarizes all the rest.

What we discover over time is that we really can't hope to fulfill The Golden Rule without putting God first and relying on His power to cleanse and guide us. We've been hurt and unwittingly learned too many of the world's ways to be consistent in our love for those around us. We also tend to have a double standard when it comes to others, similar to the two-column method of accounting that we all use naturally.

As you know, accountants place value in two columns, one for positive or good (credit) and the other for negative or bad (debit). We generalize similarly, for instance, when someone asks us how our day is going and

**Sanctified: Coming Clean With God**

we add up the positive things, subtract the negative ones, and report if the balance is up or down.

We naturally do the same for people. We count some to be more admirable and easier to love, while others have less admirable qualities that tend to put us off. And sometimes we write off entire categories of people as being less worthy of our care and attention than others. Maybe we think they did bad things or are just naturally "bad" due to their age, sex, race, language, or other marker. We don't associate with those. It's OK, we say, you can't care about everybody.

But God does, and perhaps He has even put them in our path to help us see our own shortfallings and grow in His grace. The question is, will we follow His lead and use His one-column accounting system?

*For those who love God all things work together for good, for those who are called according to his purpose.*
Romans 8:28

So how do we handle it when we encounter people that are a real trial? James, the brother of Jesus, had a formula we can apply:

*Count it all joy, my brothers, when you meet trials of various kinds, for you know that the testing of your faith produces steadfastness. And let steadfastness have its full effect, that you may be perfect and complete, lacking in nothing.*
James 1:2-4

## My Struggles to Overcome

1. Are there people in your life that you have a hard time loving or even relating to constructively?

2.  Have you, friends, or members of your family had difficulty with prejudice or unloving attitudes from or toward others?

3.  Read Luke 6:27-38. Can you identify people in your life, past or present, that you might count to be enemies?

4.  Can you think of anyone who might consider you to be an enemy because of who you are or things you've said or done?

5.  Make a list of people that you would like God's encouragement and
    guidance about reaching out to with His grace and love.

Be thorough while you're answering each question by taking notes
below as well as on additional sheets of paper or in an ongoing daily
journal of your insights, meditations, prayers, and thoughts. Don't
forget to try memorizing some Scriptures!

# Lesson 9B
# Expressing gratitude and thanksgiving

**Step 6: Communicating with God:** Reserve dedicated time with God for self-examination, Bible reading, fasting and prayer in order to know God and His will for my life and to gain the power to follow His will.

Learning to live a life of gratitude, demonstrated by my words and actions as I become more and more generous with my time and talent by giving to God and others through regular tithing and offerings.

---

We always have a choice, just like the Israelites of old who were rescued from bondage in Egypt and were on their way to the Promised land: should we be grateful or grumble?

Let's face it; life is always going to have its challenges on this side of Heaven. Our choice has to do with how we face them. Do we complain to the high heavens and those around us or do we give thanks for God's gifts of life, breath, and provision in meeting them successfully? In other words, do we take His gifts for granted and gripe about the difficulties we encounter?

In our last study we noted God's one-column approach as outlined in James 1:2-4. Take a moment to reread this passage in Lesson 8B. The same trials and tribulations that would naturally provoke complaining, although difficult and even grievous, can be used by God to strengthen our faith as we recognize and apply God's grace in each situation. We can let go of our grumbling and *"count it all joy"* using God's one column system, knowing He never leaves us nor forsakes us and doesn't ask us to endure a trial without comforting us and giving us the means to overcome it.

Thank God for His faithfulness and forgiveness, for His love and generous provision, for His guidance and protection! We've been given not only life but new life in abundance, faith and family, food and fellowship, shelter and sustenance, and all that we need. So we choose to love Him and learn to put aside (repent from) our human grievances and give Him thanks and praise through thick and thin. Then watch as He pours out his encouragement, comfort, and wisdom in the midst of our trials.

Of course, there are a lot of plainly "good" things to be grateful for that will automatically go into our "credit" column if we can just take our eyes off our old, abandoned "debit" column. The problem with keeping two columns is that the enemy of our souls is always at work trying to point out some down side so we can grumble.

OK. All that's left for us to do is figure out how many ways we can express our gratitude to God and everyone around us. A few keys:

+ Receive everything and everyone as gifts from God.
+ Make it a habit to outdo yourself in being generous with your encouragement, time, and talents to help your family and everyone around you.
+ Be generous with giving back to God through tithes and offerings both inside and outside your church.

Where will you get the means to be generous? Try Him! In the words of the old hymn: "Count your blessings; name them one by one. Count your many blessings; see what God has done."

*Whoever sows bountifully will also reap bountifully... for God loves a cheerful giver.*                                2 Corinthians 9:6-7

## My Gratitude

1.  Are you a grateful believer or a grumbler? Jot down some ways that you can replace griping with gratitude.

2. How often do you spontaneously offer encouragement or express gratitude to your family, coworkers, and others?

3. Would you characterize yourself as a cheerful giver or more practical (read "reluctant" or even "stingy") with your giving?

4. How familiar are you with the rationale and mandate behind the practice of tithing? How do you support your church?

5. How often to you help your neighbors or others you see who are in need?

6. What other ways do you share your time, talent, and treasure with those around you? Note some good results you've seen.

Be thorough while you're answering each question by taking notes below as well as on additional sheets of paper or in an ongoing daily journal of your insights, meditations, prayers, and thoughts. Don't forget to try memorizing some Scriptures!

*Rejoice always, pray without ceasing, give thanks in all circumstances; for this is the will of God in Christ Jesus for you.*   1 Thessalonians 5:16-18

Speaking of gratitude, you'll also find an interesting handout called **What About Tithing** at www.celebratesalvation.org/more.

**Step 6  Lesson 9B**

# Lesson 10B
# Daily devotions and study

**Step 6: Communicating with God:** Reserve dedicated time with God for self-examination, Bible reading, fasting and prayer in order to know God and His will for my life and to gain the power to follow His will.

Learn how to study the Word of God; institute daily devotions including prayer and journaling; and enter into regular fellowship, worship, and sharing the LORD's Supper with others of kindred Christian faith.

---

### Jesus' Parable of the Sower

*"A sower went out to sow. And as he sowed, some seeds fell along the path, and the birds came and devoured them. Other seeds fell on rocky ground, where they did not have much soil, and immediately they sprang up since they had no depth of soil, but when the sun rose they were scorched. And since they had no root, they withered away. Other seeds fell among thorns, and the thorns grew up and choked them. Other seeds fell on good soil and produced grain, some a hundredfold, some sixty, some thirty. He who has ears, let him hear."*

Matthew 13:3-9

The "seeds" in this parable refer to the living Word of God, the words of Scripture as quickened by the Holy Spirit. The soil they're planted in is our souls. We cooperate with this process when we prepare our hearts to receive God's Word by making ourselves available, opening our hearts to Him, breaking up any "fallow ground" we find there, and devoting ourselves to studying and meditating upon His Word with a desire to grow and apply it in our lives.

Developing regular times of devotion to prayerful study of and meditation on the Word of God as recorded in the Bible is a vital and necessary part of our growth in faith. It's how we learn to understand God's nature and His will for our lives.

**Sanctified: Coming Clean With God**

*But* [Jesus] *answered* [the devil], *"It is written, 'Man shall not live by bread alone, but by every word that comes from the mouth of God.'"*

Matthew 4:4 (referencing Deuteronomy 8:3)

*All Scripture is breathed out by God and profitable for teaching, for reproof, for correction, and for training in righteousness, that the man of God may be complete, equipped for every good work.*          2 Timothy 3:16-17

*For the word of God is living and active, sharper than any two-edged sword, piercing to the division of soul and of spirit, of joints and of marrow, and discerning the thoughts and intentions of the heart.*   Hebrews 4:12

Becoming a dedicated disciple of Christ is an ongoing process. If you haven't already, this is definitely the time to commit or recommit to having a dedicated time and routine for daily devotions, Bible study, meditation, prayer, and journaling. You can access helpful handouts in the **Book 1 – Saved** list at www.celebratesalvation.org/more to guide you in organizing your regular Bible study routine and setting up your daily devotional time

## My Devotional Life

1.   Have you organized and gotten settled into a pattern of regular daily devotions and Bible Study? If not, why?

2.  Are you getting comfortable with and comfort from your time in prayer and meditation?

3.  The written Word is called the *Logos*. The Holy Spirit makes it personal as the *Rhema*. Have you felt God's Word come alive?*

4.  How familiar do you feel you are with the overall Biblical testimony of God's love and the plans He has for you?

5. Are you having any difficulties with your devotional time? List some of them below.

Be thorough while you're answering each question by taking notes below as well as on additional sheets of paper or in an ongoing daily journal of your insights, meditations, prayers, and thoughts.

\* Following up on Question 3, here's another passage about the Word of God to ponder and absorb:

*And the Word became flesh and dwelt among us, and we have seen his glory, glory as of the only Son from the Father, full of grace and truth.*

John 1:14

If you're still having trouble getting going or staying committed to regular devotions and Bible study, consider looking over the **Book 1 – Saved Handouts** listed online at www.celebratesalvation.org/more.

**Step 6  Lesson 10B**

# Lesson 11B
# Becoming a Disciple

**Step 6: Communicating with God:** Reserve dedicated time with God for self-examination, Bible reading, fasting and prayer in order to know God and His will for my life and to gain the power to follow His will.

How to become a disciple by developing a habitual pattern of seeking and obedience to God's guidance and direction.

---

*Trust in the* LORD *with all your heart, and do not lean on your own understanding. In all your ways acknowledge him, and he will make straight your paths.*
                                                    Proverbs 3:5-6

According to Wikipedia, the term "disciple" represents the Koine Greek word μαθητής (*mathētēs*), which generally means "one who engages in learning through instruction from another, a pupil or apprentice." Christians are followers of the Christ (Messiah) who have decided to follow the word and example of Jesus in an earnest and disciplined way. Where does this word come from? The opening verses of John 1 can help us here:

*In the beginning was the Word, and the Word was with God, and the Word was God. He was in the beginning with God. All things were made through him, and without him was not any thing made that was made.* John 1:1-3

God the Father commissioned Jesus, the living Word of God, to speak our universe into being, Then in the fullness of time He sent this only begotten Son into our fallen world to be our Messiah, Savior, and Lord by demonstrating His patient love, mercy, and power on our behalf. Jesus came in flesh and blood *"and dwelt among us"* as a divine adoption agent to reconcile us to His Father.

We've been called into an amazing family with a loving Father who desires to build us up in a warm personal relationship. As we grow in faith or "trust" in God, we learn to appreciate the challenging truths and encouragement found in His Word.

**Sanctified: Coming Clean With God**

To paraphrase Jesus' words in Matthew 7:24-27, "Become my disciple, observe my ways, and heed my teaching and you will be like someone who has built his house on a rock so that even the storms of life won't take it down." The Holy Bible is the Word of God in written form; Jesus is the Word of God made flesh; and His Father has become our loving Father through spiritual adoption, which we live out through the discipline of discipleship.

It's true that discipline sometimes involves a degree of suffering, as any person who's been a child will affirm:

*Have you forgotten the exhortation that addresses you as sons? "My son, do not regard lightly the discipline of the Lord, nor be weary when reproved by him. For the Lord disciplines the one he loves, and chastises every son whom he receives."*

Hebrews 12:5-6 (from Proverbs 3:11-12)

But several verses on down in Hebrews 12:11 the Word of God promises that later on this discipline *"yields the peaceful fruit of righteousness to those who have been trained by it."*

May our God bless you in every way as you seek to do His will.

## My Growth as a Disciple

1.  How well do you handle the encouragement, guidance and chastisement of discipline? Can you stay focused and on task?

2. Are you seeking to become a disciple of Jesus? If so, how consistently are you studying the His Word and yielding?

3. What areas of your home, work, and personal life would you count to be well-disciplined? Which ones need work?

4. Where do you especially feel the need for God's ongoing direction, strength, and wisdom?

5. Have you experienced any of the *"peaceable fruit of righteousness"* promised by discipline yet? Describe.

6. What are your priorities in life? Number them from most to least important on the list below, first before this course and now.

| Focus | Before | Now | Comments: |
|-------|--------|-----|-----------|
| Career | _____ | _____ | |
| Family | _____ | _____ | |
| Church | _____ | _____ | |
| Christ | _____ | _____ | |
| Friends | _____ | _____ | |
| Money | _____ | _____ | |
| Ministry | _____ | _____ | |

Be thorough while you're answering each question by taking notes on additional sheets of paper or in an ongoing daily journal of your insights, meditations, prayers, and thoughts. Don't forget to share with your accountability partner and try memorizing some Scriptures!

# Lesson 12B
# Living The LORD's Prayer

**Step 6: Communicating with God:** Reserve dedicated time with God for self-examination, Bible reading, fasting and prayer in order to know God and His will for my life and to gain the power to follow His will.

Seeking first the Kingdom of God and His righteousness in every aspect of my life to ensure that His will is done and His provision is secure.

---

*Now Jesus was praying in a certain place, and when he finished, one of his disciples said to him, "Lord, teach us to pray, as John taught his disciples."*

Luke 11:1

His response was:

*"Pray then like this: our Father in heaven, hallowed be your name. Your Kingdom come, your will be done on earth as it is in heaven. Give us this day our daily bread, and forgive us our debts, as we forgive our debtors. Do not lead us into temptation, but deliver us from the evil one. For yours is the Kingdom and the power and the glory forever."*

Matthew 6:9-13

Further on in the same discourse, Jesus addressed priorities:

*"Seek first the kingdom of God and his righteousness, and all these things will be added to you."*

Matthew 6:33

When a Pharisee asked about Moses' highest priorities, He replied:

*"You shall love the Lord your God with all your heart and with all your soul and with all your mind. This is the great and first commandment. And a second is like it: You shall love your neighbor as yourself. On these two commandments depend all the Law and the Prophets."*

Matthew 22:37-40

A careful analysis of these teachings discloses the essential elements of what it means to live the life of a disciple, namely to:

1.  Love and cleave in trust to your heavenly Father.

**Sanctified: Coming Clean With God**

2. Seek His Kingdom and His perfect way of living.

3. Receive forgiveness and turn with forgiveness to share His love with all around you, leaning on His power to carry out His will in your life.

People puzzle about what "righteousness" is. It seems to me one of those words that have become so "religious" that any practical sense of application has been lost. However, it simply means to "live in right relationship with God, your fellow human beings, and all of God's surrounding creation."

Growing in righteousness is essentially what it takes to be an active citizen in the Kingdom of a King who seeks perfect love, liberty, family, harmony, education, politics, climate control, you name it. Only God can do it, but He invites us to join Him in becoming part of the solution instead of part of the problem by developing daily, hour-by-hour, minute-by-minute, sensitivity and obedience to His loving guidance, support, and empowerment.

O Lord, please let your Kingdom come and your will be done on earth as it is in heaven! Simply said, living The Lord's Prayer in the power of His Holy Spirit is what the yielded life of a disciple is all about.

## My Obedience

1. We have "Gethsemane struggles" whenever our will comes up against God's. What struggles of this kind do you deal with?

2.  In a few sentences below, what is your definition of the Gospel of the Kingdom?

3.  How have you been "seeking first the Kingdom of God and His righteousness"?

4.  Do you think it's possible to be successful in fulfilling the "second commandment" without pursuing the first?

5.  Make a prayerful list below of the areas in your life that you're seeking God's help with as you complete this study, then come back to it from time to time and note your progress.

Be thorough while you're answering each question by taking notes below as well as on additional sheets of paper or in an ongoing daily journal of your insights, meditations, prayers, and thoughts. Don't forget to try memorizing some Scriptures!

This is a good topic to close our second booklet with, since we're going to be taking an in-depth look at the Kingdom of God and how to share the Good News about it in Word, Deed, and Power in our third study coming up.

As you prepare to move deeper into the Joy of Discipleship, you may appreciate reading a short book by C. S. Lewis entitled **The Four Loves**, available as a PDF at www.celebratesalvation.org/more. Lewis' analysis of the different manifestations of love is very helpful in overcoming the confusion attached to the word in today's world.

# Commendation

Congratulations! You've just completed our study of what it is to enter into and participate actively in God's loving plan not only to make your life whole as you dedicate it to Him but to keep it that way by cleansing, purifying, and enriching it so that you can live and bear fruit in every good work.

*For the grace of God has appeared, bringing salvation for all people, training us to renounce ungodliness and worldly passions, and to live self-controlled, upright, and godly lives in the present age, waiting for our blessed hope, the appearing of the glory of our great God and Savior Jesus Christ, who gave himself for us to redeem us from all lawlessness and to purify for himself a people for his own possession who are zealous for good works.*      Titus 2:11-14

Let's keep it up together with Him as we continue to grow while we investigate in our next study guide, ***Sent: Becoming a Living Letter***, what is involved in being sent as His ambassadors into our broken and fallen world.

May our LORD and Savior continue to bless, favor, encourage, and sanctify you for service in His Kingdom!

*Now to him who is able to keep you from stumbling and to present you blameless before the presence of his glory with great joy, to the only God, our Savior, through Jesus Christ our Lord, be glory, majesty, dominion, and authority, before all time and now and forever. Amen.*      Jude 1:24-25

# Suggestions for Further Study

**The Holy Bible**
*English Standard Version® ESV Study Bible™.*

**Samuel Bagster family**
*Daily Light on the Daily Path.* Morning and evening Bible verses.

**Henry T. Blackaby**
*Experiencing God: Knowing* and *Doing the Will of God.*

**James Choung**
*Real Life: A Christianity Worth Living Out.*

**Richard J. Foster**
*Celebration of Discipline: The Path to Spiritual Growth.*

**C. S. Lewis**
*How to Pray: Reflections and Essays* and *The Four Loves.*

**Watchman Nee**
*Sit, Walk, Stand.*

**A. J. Russell**
*For Sinners Only.*

**Ann Voskamp**
*One Thousand Gifts Devotional* and *The Broken Way.*

**Dallas Willard**
*Renovation of the Heart: Putting On the Character of Christ.*
*Hearing God: Developing a Conversational Relationship with God.*

# Additional Celebrate Salvation® Resources

## Books in the Joy of Christian Discipleship Series

### *The Joy of Christian Discipleship Course 1*
Established in 3 Stages and 7 Steps, a 36-week group study

1. **Stage A – Saved!** *Rescued by Grace*

2. Stage B – Sanctified: *Coming Clean with God* (this book)
   **Stage B Handouts** *****
   What is an *"-ism"*?
   Life Survey Worksheet (1B)
   Family History Worksheet (1B)
   Spiritual Life Survey Worksheet (2B)
   Interpersonal Worksheet (Helps) (3B)
   Interpersonal Worksheet (Hurts) (3B)
   Stewardship Survey Worksheet (4B)
   Periodic Review Worksheet (6B)
   What About Tithing? (9B)

3. **Stage C – Sent:** *Becoming a Living Letter*

   **Plus – Handouts and Worksheets** or **Complete Course 1**

### *Devotional Guide to 3 Stages and 7 Steps* *****

4. **Essentials of the Christian Faith**
   7 Steps to Abundant Life, a 7-week daily devotional guide

### *The Joy of Christian Discipleship Course 2* *****
Equipped with Understanding, a 36-week group study

5. **Awakening:** *The Triumph of Truth*

6. **Kingdom:** *God's Reign in our Midst*

7. **Heaven:** *Our Ultimate Destiny*

   **Plus – Handouts and Worksheets** or **Complete Course 2**

***** Links to all handouts in printable PDF form as well as suggested books and information about Additional Resources can be found online at www.celebratesalvation.org/more. Books 4-7 are under development at the time of this publication.

CPSIA information can be obtained
at www.ICGtesting.com
Printed in the USA
BVHW010753130321
602276BV00016B/1270